My Life of Poems

My Life of Poems

Poetic Outlets of True Life and Abstracts

DWIGHT A. BLOODMAN

Foreword by Betty-Ann Bloodman

RESOURCE *Publications* · Eugene, Oregon

MY LIFE OF POEMS
Poetic Outlets of True Life and Abstracts

Resource Publications
An Imprint of Wipf and Stock Publishers
199 W. 8th Ave., Suite 3
Eugene, OR 97401

www.wipfandstock.com

PAPERBACK ISBN: 978-1-6667-6626-4
HARDCOVER ISBN: 978-1-6667-6627-1
EBOOK ISBN: 978-1-6667-6628-8

01/16/23

This poem book is naturally dedicated to my Lord and Savior Jesus Christ, my wife Betty-Ann, and daughters Azariah and Cassia.

This is due to the fact that it is truly snapshots of my life from childhood, teenage years, adulthood, marriage, walk with The Creator and beyond 'SERVED ON POETIC PLATES'. They all are primarily the source and passion from which my poems are dictated.

May we all go on to higher heights and deeper depts together.

If I never see you again,
make sure I see you in Heaven.

CONTENTS

CONTENTS

CONTENTS

FOREWORD

God has given everyone a purpose to fulfill in life and my husband has been gifted with words. He has expressed most of his life through the art of writing poetry. Knowing him for over twenty years I have seen him at his lowest and highest moments. Some persons use different tools or strategies to overcome in life, but using his God given ability to write has allowed him to experience true freedom from every bondage and led to greater opportunities. Throughout his life Dwight has taken the curveballs thrown at him to propel him to the next level.

The content of the poems written are not just mere words, but sincere thoughts from his innermost being. They are captivating and will speak to your heart and bring transformation; encouraging you to put off the old man which is corrupt and be renewed in the spirit.

Mrs. Betty-Ann Bloodman

"ALL I SEE"

Every one of us would love to have the perfect mate,
That is all I see in Betty-Ann Mommy Brenda.
Where was I when Betty-Ann was born?
When she cried for whatever reason,
I did not comfort her, change her,
Or told her it would be ok. You did!
You have taught her to be a woman by the grace of God.
You have taught her how to build her house,
And not tear it down with her hands!
How to love God, how to love her husband,
How to love meee!
But I was not there; I did not see these things,
I could not have been there.

Thank you Mommy Brenda for Betty-Ann Bloodman.
I am 'unaware' of the Process that made her who she is today.
The Perfect Help Meet- The Finished Product:
Productive, Beautiful, Godly—That Is All I See!

Inspiration and/or reason:

'All I See' complements my mother-in-law for raising her daughter to be such 'wife material'. Written to be ready at our wedding among other compositions we read and sang to each other. It was short of a wedding musical lol.

A GENTLE BREEZE

You're a gentle breeze, upon my knees
You're a silent wind, upon my chin
What I mean, this I say
You make me feel great every day.

You're a firm twig in the ground, as this mountain I climb
You're a rock in place, as I run this race
What I mean, this I say
You help me find my way—everyday.

You're my body, my spirit & soul
You're the one I touch, I merge, I hold
What I mean, this I say
You're my wife and Happy Birthday.

Inspiration and/or reason:

'A Gentle Breeze' is a love poem to my wife about being a complimenting to me. Inspiration came when I saw a picture of a lone twig of a plant on a hill.

A MOTHER TO ME

She is not only the mother of our Zar' & Cass'
But Betty you're like a mother to me
The way you stay up late and rise up early
You care for our daughters and still remember time for me
How you do it is still a mystery.
Can anyone blame me if I say I love you?
Can you blame me if I honor you and say,
Happy Mother's Day?

Inspiration and/or reason:

'A Mother To Me' was a Mother's Day poem to wife. It depicts a wise, industrious woman.

A MOTHER'S LOVE

Nothing short of the Agape love,
Is a Mother's love.
When I was born she was there,
To cuddle me near.
She picked me up when I fell -
Made sure I was well.

She taught me about Jesus,
Even when I could not read or spell,
And stared me away from hell.
She wiped my tears when I cried,
And said, "It is OK I have tried."

Sometimes I awe,
For the dept of a Mother's Love I saw.
For even when I am bad,
She nurtures me although she is sad.

Nothing destroys a Mother's love,
It is unconditional; it is pure,
Like God's Love it is Sure.

Inspiration and/or reason:

'A Mother To Me' is a general Mother's Day poem. Was written for all the good mothers out there.

A NEW REALM OF LOVE

Whole new realm of love appears and overcome us
As roses unfolds layer by layer revealing their beauty.
That moment in time is not known to me,
When I'm virtually alone with you baby.
Are you real my love?
Are you a miracle in front of me?

This waist, it gently touches and kisses my eyes,
This body, let me always be the one
To engulf it with love intents.
We need to run wild and free
Tempestuous furnaces of passion for our morning tea
To smelt and purify the ore of love
Between you and me
Alone this God set path of our destiny.

We need to converse,
For conversation is closer than talk.
If I could not behold your beauty,
What would become of me?
For you dictate these lines,
By the lovely "umm" I see.

I have the best, you guys may take the rest,
But look out world, I've got the best girl!
She has talent beyond compare,
Whispering love to me by ear!

She places her heart in the clouds for me to see,
And reflects her face in the moonlight at night,
Just to say "I love you Dwight"!

"I love you _____, you're wholly beautiful."
I'm c-arrested for loving you,
And sentenced to a life of marriage, happiness too.
But do you know why I said you're beautiful?
"Because you are."
And why do I say I love you
"Because I do"
You're now about to say, "I love you too"

Inspiration and/or reason:

'A New Realm Of Love' is a description of a transition point in love when you know it is real and deep. Breaking up now would hurt badly. Healing will take a long time.

A ROSE

A freshly cut rose symbolizes love, trust, and honor
Its components entail the very fabric of love
It is a metaphor of a heart filled with love
And wonder, for it blooms when it's fed
And like the rose, if the heart is not fed
With "Love expressions" it soon fades away
But time is the healer of all things
Because of this, new roses germinate out of the bed of your heart
As a symbol of undying love.

But the artificial rose represents love without life,
Give either to someone, and you imply its contents to that person.

Inspiration and/or reason:

'A Rose' was birthed out of my despising giving artificial flowers. It
explores the meaning I give behind giving a real versus a fake rose.

A SUBSTITUTE FOR ME

Receive this gift with love I pray
For I give you with all of my heart
With it ohh! How I would love to say,
Because I care for you
Here is something that will share with you—the quiet, happy moments
The sad.
It's purrs that will cheer you up when you're down
Just doing my job when I'm not around.
And whatever they or I can't do
I pray that God will fix for you.
Again, just because I care
Here is something huggable, loveable, and kind
The closest gift to substitute me
That I could find.

Inspiration and/or reason:

'A Substitute For Me' is about a gift sent to keep my then girlfriend company. We have it to this day but no need for it to substitute anymore lol.

ALL MY LIFE

I have I have
been looking all my been looking all my
life for you! Do you life for you! Do you love
love me, can this work? me, can this work? Yes I like
Yes I like you and I love you! I you and I love you!
love you so much let us ask God Yes let us ask God!
about this! It is God's will, Betty Yes Dwight I will
be my girlfriend! We, be your girlfriend! We
commend in every way! Your commend in
Family & friends love me! every way!
Dove of my life! Yours love me
I will be too! Love of my
your husband life! I
am your wife!
I LOVE
YOU

.

Inspiration and/or reason:

'All My Life' (and Lord Forgive Me For Loving Like This) heart-shaped poems are poetic not only in words but in their physical shape structure as well, i.e., heart shaped. They depict two people or hearts or souls coming together in conversation firstly. Speaking back and forth to each other. Realizing stages in love at the same time. As we also come together in soul, in heart, in spirit and of the body in marriage until we merge as one in every way, and you cannot tell us apart. This is what happened between my wife and

I. 'All My Life' covers the period of deciding if she is the one. The funny thing is, one the other side (of the heart shape and in reality) she was trying to decide as well. Eventually it all came together in the end.

AS A VULPINE

1

I am almost afraid to write this poem,
For I know it can reach into the crevices of my heart,
Releasing emotions of love, fear, hurt, longings.
I mean, I have such tremendous love, God inspired love;
One that is full, joyous, wonderful and creative.
But I may never be able to share it with that special person.

2

What! You may ask, what inhibits your love?
My past I would reply.
It is there-lingering in the shadow of doubt,
And could be conclusively, everlastingly terminal to 'love'.
For in Heaven there is no 'ultimate intimacy',
No marriage, no procreation,
Imagine no releasing of myself to engulf that special one in complete unrestrained love. . .

3

So I shun them; their ever-elevating outreach,
Their curiosity about my mystery,
I shun their love and recoil from their friendship,
I just can't endorse myself as a Christian with the shadow of doubt,
Then I think—WHEN if ever will I know that endocrine manifestation?
Will I ever give or receive that clasping endemic of lips?

I could you know—I can release myself; FROM-THE-STIGMA. . .
But then hope is redressed with the lingering shadow,
It's there—it's just ever presently there; AS A VULPINE. . .

Inspiration and/or reason:

'As A Vulpine' is a description of a fear I had that could have caused me not to be able to have a relationship nor marry. In the end the fear turned out to be false and toothless.

AS I SAY HAPPY BIRTHDAY

In all the world I can't find
A phenomenon so mysterious to the human mind.
The birth of a young lady is so wonderful
It contains promises that are extremely bountiful.
But the only way you are going to capture every opportunity
Is to place your hand, in the hand of the almighty
And what better time, as I say:

> Happy Birthday!

Inspiration and/or reason:

'As I Say Happy Birthday' is a short poem **as part of** my wife's, then girlfriend's **Birthday gifts.** Yes, I do this kind of thing for almost every occasion, whether an official one or not.

BETTY

Sweet
Beautiful
Luscious
Sexy
Godly
Loving
Quiet
Proud
Firm
Helper
Homemaker
Neat
Compact
Lovely
Small
Petite
Dynamic
Tempestuous
Bold
Bright
Prosperous
Spiritual
Caring
Ravishing
Rude
Ready
Ripe

Round
Betty. . .

Inspiration and/or reason:

'Betty' is a **single word per line poem description** of my wife. I've found the greater and more impactful a person is, the more perfectly one-word descriptions represent that person.

"BETTY DON'T LET ME LOVE AGAIN"

When you realize you want to spend the rest of your life with someone
You want the rest of your life to start as soon as possible
Betty you are that someone.

When you realize God have given you his best
You want to give your best to him & others
Betty let's give our best baby.

When life have been re-started for you sooo many times
You want to find that special place of finality
Betty I do not want to lose you.

When all you have dreamed of and prophecy is before you
You want things to become legal—yours forever
Betty don't let me love again.

Inspiration and/or reason:

'Betty Don't Let Me Love Again' expresses, bellows a deep desire
to settle down. After going through the trenches of past relation-
ships, yes you want to settle down.

BLACK HISTORY IS HISTORY

1

Black History month is History,
But that's not good enough for me.
Did Martin Luther King Jr dream come through?
Or is the fulfillment of it YOU?
Is a memorial month what Carter G. Woodson intended,
Or to push pass 1926 would he be offended?

2

Yes we built the pyramids with great 'power',
Our accomplishments as tall as the Babel tower.
If Madam C.J. Walker's hair was the 1st Millionaire there,
How can we become Billionaires-Trillionaires here?
Don't dwell too much on the past, it does not last.

Think present, continue the trend; innovate-create, make your dent,
Please don't be like some who only vent!

Inspiration and/or reason:

'Black History Is History' is a Black history month poem written for one of my daughters homework. It **acknowledges contributors** of the past, **but** it **more importantly** points us to continuing to build a future, together.

CHARM

The gifts and gold
Does good not harm,
But I use words to charm.
Like:
Roses are red, white, and yellow, with violets being blue.
But the only delicate flower I want to hold is you.
Because I loved you once, I now love you twice,
I love you. . .
Because you're wholesomely loving, very nice.
That is why I can see time is the space between you and me.

Inspiration and/or reason:

'Charm' is a poem of **anticipation** . . . I knew time will tell and time told. . .

DELUSION

I

In one night you loose everything,
Where are they, the love, smiles, affection?
What killed them?
Are these sightings, moods and urges designed for this?
Yeah I'm supposed to be happy, but I'm Sad,
I try to enjoy mingling but the heartache,
The heartache of the original afflictive blessing is molding me,
One night, just one night and here comes victorious gloom.

2

Will there ever be that Godly happiness. . .
As I conceived from the Holy Spirit; and want?
I don't know; my vision is limited to what is before me,
If only I had the chance to communicate my emotions and knowledge.

3

One thing was good though, as far as my perception permits-
An ultimatum, what I want is too much for "the world" to give,
So I will 'forever' refine myself to person—self and one focus . . .
I will live for God despite these afflictions.

4

The bustle hurts my eyes,
Confined laughter does numbers to my eyes,
Now I am confused to wonder,
For everything seems foreign to me.
Or do I have to compete?—I don't think so!
The lamb that is lost; if it is mine; will return.
I now declare Satan to be a liar and leave that which is to be sober
in Jesus' name!

5

God! How do I throw away such burning anguish?
Doth a spiritual fire stop burning?
How do I rejoin the social?
I invite them to peek in, it's empty—my heart!
It's emotionally drained. What else can I do or say?
I don't need 'them' anymore anyway,
Then again, they are there, but just inactive.

6

If I exercise the suppressed one; someone will notice.
Now I must keep 'myself' away from them.
For desires can flare easily only to be stifled by these 'memories',
Such that a man cannot bare alone.
For there are a lot of reconstruction and renovating of my heart due.
But they can't help me, for they are blind to my figurative position. . .
When I concentrate I will achieve it; I'm sure.

Maybe a miracle will take place,
But that is not my concern now.
The dust and flare will settle, hysteria will be calm,
Those concerned will regret when it's too late; can't say I did not try.
And each response was a lie!
This is now my steal wall, nothing gets in!
And IF nothing comes in the box of priceless, intangible items; nothing can come out.
It is now just my God, me and school—THE NEW LOVE TRIANGLE...

Inspiration and/or reason:

'Delusion' a poem of **disappointment in how I was neglected and scorned**, by my then girlfriend, at a social.

DISTANCES IN LOVE

As we cover distances in love
New destinations become due.
As you walk deeper in love with me
And I with you.

Inspiration and/or reason:

'Distances In Love' is a short, snappy poem as we went through courtship.

DON'T FIGHT

Sitting around
My heart pounds.
No matter what I do
I think of you.
I dream at night
Of you, love, and Dwight.
So, there is no reason to fight
You're about to be loved right.

Inspiration and/or reason:

'Don't Fight' is **setting down your guards in love** when it is the right one. Many people ruin a potentially great relationship of whatever type due to unfounded prejudices from past relationships.

DREAM TO REALITY

I had a dream
Even before I graced my eyes on you
Before I saw first light
Before conception or when they named me Dwight
Before God by his might said, "Let there be light."

A tangible dream it was
My destiny
And as I read this poem
This spitting beauty of a dream is before me.

And today. . .
I have a dream that some day
This dream will be reality
Glorious, eternal, bountiful as the stars.

But can one choose from the stars of the sky?
A choice has been made
How can this be?
There are so many beautiful stars out there,
To compare—mind boggling to me.

Perhaps the dream was God's perfect destiny
For us to become one
Under the title of Mr & Mrs. Bloodman.

Inspiration and/or reason:

'Dream To Reality' is a figurative **love dream to reality.** Everything starts in the mind. Desire, and dynamic plans and actions draws it out into physical reality (not just spiritual).

EVERY BREATH IS YOURS"

In 2002 I met you,
2004 culminated in love galore,
And today I love you even more.

For sure difficulty came,
Yet your strength, beauty and love for me rained.
So this day I maintain;
Every breath is YOURS . . .
My body, my spirit, my soul,
To love you unconditionally is my goal.

(EVERY BREATH IS YOURS")

So today my sweet Betty',
Relax on the cushion of my thoughts,
As I say, I LOVE YOU baby.
I give my all to you again,
From now until I reach Heaven.

Inspiration and/or reason:

'Every Breath Is Yours' is an **expression of devoted love.** For this
level of unconditional love, Every Breath Is Yours. . .It was origi-
nally written to be printed on two sides of a folded card. Hence the
instructions "continued on next side."

FAST & PRAY

This knowledge is so heavy, burdensome
It slows me into a time wrap
Of silence suspended in still, dark, slow procession.
I watch myself suspended, marveling
Yet I know! the solution to this is simple.

You say your sister is ungrateful.
She wants the mother role so young
How dear she speaks to me that way.
You'll pay for breaking the regulation skin I placed on you.

And you reply with closed eyes
Remove this skin
It itches when I try to move
And it is too tight
I have outgrown it.
Besides, it's your personal tradition.
Now I command the chaos to stop
The dust to settle.
I am sick of it, and you share the same emotion
Whether you know it or not.

It is simple, fast and pray
Then brother eventually turn the right way
You too will be able to say
"I love you"
In a new, special, powerful verb

While performing what potential
Was committed to that word.

Inspiration and/or reason:

'Fast & Pray' written as the **solution to a problem.** Big sister and brother were the substitute parents. But the 'sister-child' is grown now . . .

"FIRST THOUGHT I KNEW"

The first thought I knew, of you . . .
You passed a dollar through school wall,
I felt important and tall
Though I was small.

We were brothers; I felt your love,
One good thing in you from above.

Now I pray, osmosis justice.
Now I pray, you had time to say,
Jesus save me, that we may see you again . . .
Some day!

Inspiration and/or reason:

'First Thought I Knew', written **to commemorate one of my brothers.** My 'first' memory of a role model big brother was very loving. Although he had some negative issues, he loved all his family and longed for our father.

GOD KNEW

God Knew
What He created you to do and what you would do
What He created you to see and what you would see
Don't blame He . . .

Don't justify, a lie
Don't be bogged down and tie
Don't retreat and always flee
For with Him, you win on your knee.

So let's go forward, let's see,
Live another second, another minute
Another hour, another day,
Live I say, the right way . . .

And you will overcome, prosper, and fulfill,
All the glorious things (you must), according to His Will!

Inspiration and/or reason:

'God Knew' gives **hope and assurance** to move forward in Purpose.
God knew all you would have and will encounter. So, you got this. . .

GOD'S OPPORTUNITY

This is your pain
You need to be touched
You need to be held.
You exhale—your body throbs for me
I am Delayed. . .
I feel your pain.
It cries out in your voice
Desperate, Loving, Encouraging
I Want you; I Desire you
To Indulge—To Kiss you, to Hug you.
But I look straight ahead
That Day will be Great.
God knows your pain
This is His Opportunity
As We Humble on the Knee
He will come through for You & Me
"I LOVE YOU BETTY."

Inspiration and/or reason:

'God's Opportunity' holds back passionate intimacy until marriage with God's help.

HAPPY BIRTHDAY OUR QUEEN

I want to wish Happy Birthday to the Love Of My Life,
My wife, my friend, my lover, a mother,
We prefer her over every other.

So Happy Birthday to the Queen Of our Hearts,
After we knew you 'swhen' life truly start,
And you my love is the best part.

And enjoy each moment Mother of Our Princesses,
Our lives together have stood the 'test-is',
Because of YOU we know what the bes' is.

Inspiration and/or reason:

'Happy Birthday Our Queen' . . . as the self-appointed yet well de-
sired **Queen of the house** this poem was written for my wife and
mother of our children. Happy Birthday from your husband and
children to our Queen.

HI BABY,

I Love You _____.

My heart was filled with you today—as always honey. My longing to hold you, to touch you and just to be near _____ is too much for me to just think about. It must be done!

Today I imagined we were walking towards one another slowly. The road was narrow, white silhouette for a background, your hair blowing gently in the wind. Oh the longing we both feel until our skins starts to attract like magnets of opposite poles.

You could not stand it anymore, so you whisper a gentle kiss in the wind to me. I received it, its 'taste'—makes me want you more. It replenishes my body, my love, and my desire for you.

The rocking of your shoulders as you walk to me touched me and warmed my heart. Why did you tease me with that slender waist and those swaying hips? Don't you know I am 'just-a-man'—baby I cannot resist you.

How graceful you walk to me. Oooh baby!!! Just the thought of you walking to me. . . just the thought.

This is my woman, graceful legs, beautiful, young, sweet, elegant, intelligent. I must give it up to you for how wonderful you make me feel. Your reward will have your body in ecstasy.
I am yours baby and yours only. Let us do something about it.

Let it always be you every day in my 'thoughts'. . .

Let us get. . . . .

I Love You

_____.

Inspiration and/or reason:

'Hi Baby' hints marriage proposal & progression in love & court-ship. Here the man sees his woman deeper, and closer as they futuristically move closer and closer to each other until he almost but ask her to marry him.

HI THERE

Hi there most exotic one,
Why do you not see, yet thine eyes are open
Do you not feel it's presence, and I let you keep it?
When will you hear, my actions are shouting?
Smell that sweet aroma, that of my gentleness
Taste, please taste the mouthful-watering future
One so attractive.
But I can say you're wonderful, graceful, elegant
Full of beatitudes, kind and loving
I can also say for every title it's worth
I appreciate "You"

Inspiration and/or reason:

'Hi There' seeks to open her eyes to my love actions and her virtues.
Sometimes what we need is right in front us and we do not see.

I AM

I am a heart miner,
Thus, I unearth the treasures of your heart.

I am a tailor of hearts,
Thus, I clothe your heart with the fabrics of love.

I am your heart's artist,
Thus, I paint beautiful scenes to be stored on the walls of your
heart.

I am your heart's cushion,
Thus, our love can tread through TOUGH terraces.

I am a cobbler of hearts,
Thus, I mend your broken heart with love.

I am a metaphor of love,
Thus, a stream of passion flows through my heart,
Picking up nutrients of love from the banks which stretches wide
and deep,
To rejuvenate at my lips -
Where they can be tapped by YOURS!

Inspiration and/or reason:

'I Am' highlights my tender loving care for her (heart), along with
the love and passion that comes with it.

"I AM ANGRY!"

My voice Pierces
Like good massage oil
Like 'I love you' as I close in for a kiss.
Now like the noon sun in the desert
A sword meant to kill.
How can we live in lies?
I tear with anger for lies
Something is not clear, is it lies?
I just want to know
Don't tell me the sweet
Tell me the truth.
I love you, I just want the truth
I don't know the voice of a lion
I hate the voice of a lie-on.
Look at us at the point of marriage
Now I must decide
You lied to me?
And I am Angry!

Inspiration and/or reason:

'I am Angry' pours out from anger which burned about as hot as love because of what seems to be a lie or lies from her. This happened before marriage, and it hurt, but it was quenched.

I AM READY FOR LOVE

Song plays,
'I am ready for love'.
Beckons to that knowledge deep within me,
Calls out what I knew already.
Moving picture to my mother lights glows.
Computer gently, painfully, anticipatorily plays:
I Am Ready for Love.
It oozes out of my heart and flesh and mind and everythin'
I remember you darling.
Oh my God rescue me, what a wonder person for me-
I Am Ready for Love,
I Love You Lord
I Love Betty,
Then tears flow, I cry
Can't anyone hear me?
I stress, I Am Ready for Love!
Who can I tell, who will listen?
Who can do something about it?
Why isn't anyone doing something?
I Am Ready for Love, I Am Ready For Love!!!
Lord Let it be, she loves You, she loves me,
She Is Ready For Love, I Am Ready For Love.
Will you take me, I am ready?
Please give me your heart.
Ready To Love,
Ready to be Loved,
Ready to be touched.

Ready to be Hugged,
Ready to be Totally Intimate.
Ready to give ourselves mind, body, Soul, and Spirit.
I love you Betty I have never felt so ready to Love,
To take you in ways that you never imagined possible.
A Degree of Heaven is Our Demonstration of Love.
Love me Betty, I am ready to Love,
Don't hide from me; don't be shy.
I will reach out to you to draw you unto myself,
I will do my best; I will take my time.
Holding your hands I will show you,
Things you never felt before.
Passion, patience, persistence, hours—love.
Finally, it's here; it is done,
So many weddings attended; never our own.
So many babies looked after; never our own.
I want our own baby Betty,
I Am Ready for Love.
I Am Anointed by the thought of a baby,
Want almost need baby so, so much.
Thought of you pregnant is inviting anticipation,
I would love to see you pregnant for me.
With our baby you will look so adorable.
To live with you married—beautiful,
To be a family- I am ready For Love.
Ready to receive you- will you take me Betty?
I will take you—I take you
Betty-Ann Esther Balfour (Bloodman).
The days count down—I am ready,
You know I am ready don't you?
With all the women in the World,
I got the Best One.

You may not tell by my speech,
If only you could see my face- my heart,
Touch my spirit and soul,
I am ready for Love,
We are ready for Love.

Inspiration and/or reason:

'I Am Ready For Love' is inspired by the song 'Ready For Love' by India Arie. It shows I have all the necessary things to enter a marital union, e.g., body, soul, and spirit, a Job, we courted, had pre-marital counselling etc. So at the top of my voice, let's get married!

I COULD SAY MANY THINGS
BUT I MISS YOU

I put all my tears to pen
My weeping in your poems
Squeeze them, they drip with water.
I. . .. .
Don't know what to say.
Ha, a man of details
Could explain. . . say many thins
Ah. . .I just miss you; I miss you.
Painful
Our hearts open more for each other everyday
We see less of each other every day.
I could say many thins. . .
I miss you Baby. . .I miss you Baby
No other words are more powerful right now
No other words are more effective.
Until I see you, after I am with you, I miss you
Until the day we are One. . . then
I am with you Betty-Ann Bloodman.

Inspiration and/or reason:

'**I Could Say Many Things But I Miss You**' is inspired by my girl-friend and I who had an overseas relationship and a lot of catching up to do. But in all the things I could have said, the most important at the time being overwhelmed with passion and excitement was to simply say, "I miss you." We reached the place where we've completed all the other levels of love. The next step is really needed.

"I DID NOT WANT"

i did not want you
to cry for me when we part
i had just enjoyed your friendship.
i did not want you to fall for me
i said my God look at me!
what have I gotten myself into?
i teased the situation
now you love me
that was not supposed to happen!
you are in love with me—huhhh. . .

Today. . .

I want to be with you forever
I sorrow when we part
Greatly anticipate our wedding.
I want us to be one in love—we are
I say now, my God smile upon us!
Is it not by your will we are one?
We accept your will
Now thus our love triangle
This is how it is supposed to be!
We are in love in Christ—yes. . .

Inspiration and/or reason:

'i did not want' is written from a humble position expressed even in the way the title is written. It is about finding love when you least expect it, or you are not looking. This is when you know you are ready; when you know you do not have to. . .

I KNOW

I know!
Sometimes you wonder and worry
Having to tell me so many times sorry
I know!
If you truly love me
You'll wonder in your heart
Will the next letdown be the last?
Will the love nectar be tasted and past?
Know this once more and for the last
Hide it in your future, your present
And in every body part
Especially your heart
"I love you."
Despite your infirmity, you remain more precious to me
The cartilage that protects my knee
Words cannot express
Nevertheless, you're the best.
A name in which I can meaningfully say hi,
At night it's my lullaby.
You are my black princess
A taste of your love placed my question to rest
Yet you're my queen, the future through Eph 5:21, I have seen.
So, sweetness, as you awake
Take this from me.
I love you, Love Sponge
And you will always be
Precious to me. . .

Inspiration and/or reason:

'I Know' calms the nerve of your partner with assurances that no matter what either of you do, you will never leave them. My then girlfriend was concerned about this because of personal issues and her family past.

I LIKE POEMS

I like poems that make me laugh
Those that mystify simplicity
From an emotional crest to a trough.
I like poems—synthesizes of geomorphology
Of moods, life, events tangible and illusive.
I like fast poems,
I like them slow.
Those pitched high,
Those pitched low.
Like long poems,
Like them short.
Like to write them,
Or when I'm being taught.
Now this poem carries a moral of this sort,
I like all poems. . .
As conclusive thought.

Inspiration and/or reason:

'I Like Poems' was written because I realized yes, I like poems. I like how they allowed me to vent happiness, sadness, and abstract stuff whether any of the categories where real or fictitious and/or exploratory. Also, sometimes, I just pushed myself into the frame of mind to experience the emotions and write about them while there, whether something is happening physically, or mentally or not. This is something you MUST be VERY CAREFUL about though, because the mind does NOT know the difference.

I LISTENED TO YOUR VOICE

I listened to your voice as it changed
I listen as it speaks. . .
Saying stay firm in Christ
Be humble and grow swiftly spiritually.
Never be timid rather be bold
Be bold according as our tenet. . .
I listen and detect that tone
One that says
"We are everlasting friends."
Let us execute that rare interaction
Christ mimicking, pooling our resources
For it would be vain to keep a finite friend.

I listen and it urges me on
It's happy as a child of God should be
As estuary of everlasting holiness
A whirlwind of joy.
It is ripe, full for the ears to hear
Worthy of vibrating the ear
Worthy of entering, of saturating hearts
Worthy to utter words
And the medium proudly carry.

Now listen to my voice as it replied,
Listen as it speaks. . .
I appreciate your friendship
Cherishing your inspired voice

Adorning myself with your instructions.
I will remember your strong influence
Now, promise me that you'll stay
Come every Christmas Day.

Inspiration and/or reason:

'I Listened To Your Voice' was written for Christmas because I pick up on non-verbal communication very easily. So I was able to use all the non-verbal messages, merge them with her words and determine what she is really saying.

"I LOVE YOU TOO"

I can feel the cold breeze of your love for me
How easily you give and give and give.

I measure not your love by what you can give me
But the way you give says "I've got-to satisfy my man!!!"

I know you feel proud of me
I feel, I see your thoughts.

Thoughts of . . .
Love happiness.

When last have I been this relaxed?
The happiest I have been since. . .

Ohhh Christmas breeze
Great anticipation of joy.

Ohhh my Love
Great anticipation of joy.

O the agony, the pain of missing you
I see it baby, you Love me.

With you I see it
Closer view.

You Love me and it is tangible
A new revelation hourly, daily.

Two lines each
Two people separated.

We reach out but too far
We reach out and we are near.

Who have played this cruel joke?
Can man be so heartless?

Today I don't understand. . .
You Love me.

" . . .."
" . . .."

Thank you Betty
"i love you too"

Inspiration and/or reason:

'I Love You Too' was written around a Christmas. I was amazed by how she loves me and how she shows it. And yes, cold breeze is soothing when it flows over a person hot with good anticipation.

I NEVER TOLD YOU

I never told you the truth about me loving you
Many years ago, I loved a girl dearly.
A childhood love so powerful that it's still with me
I found myself in those days mimicking her cute ways.
I mean, she was so close to me
That I was acting like I am her actual body
Unconsciously.
You have that same effect on me
Today in church, I was dancing, praising God
And I just stopped as I realized
Beyond Simplicity
I was dancing like you
And feet like you—not me.

Inspiration and/or reason:

'I Never Told You' is perfectly positioned after 'I Love You Too' because 'I Love You Too' hinted on past relationship(s) that ended bad. 'I Never Told You' adds another piece of that puzzle and shows that I found someone who I have such a connection with again.

"I REMEMBER"

I remember, I'm romantic . . .

Years have passed,
I've begun to do the first things last,
The little sweet things and the joy they bring,
So powerful, produced a ring.

Oh the joy, the environment could have been,
The attraction of the pinnacle,
Makes my cells start tingling.

Focused romance, attention, private time,
Makes life smooth as a rhyme,
Dropped the ball terribly; but this time. . .

This time . . . in the month of December,
I remember; Oh God I remember!
I remember; Oh Betty-Ann I remember!

I remember; baby Bellae I remember,
This time to make it stick,
I Am Romantic . . .

Inspiration and/or reason:

'I Remember' was written as a kind of promise to revive my romantic side. After years in a relationship you can start taking each other for granted. To keep a relationship growing and happy, both persons must continue doing things 'like' what they did in the beginning that their spouse loved.

I WAS LONELY

i was Lonely and alone
When i heard "In the Chill of the night."
i was lonely
I was amazed that God who made all I see
God, that God made me.
i had no one, no one to love
it was not despair; it was a peaceful realization
that God is in control.
I knew that someday He would find me somebody
and today I love You.
How wonderful the pain of your anticipation!
So powerful I knew it had to be great
Betty you meeting me was simply fate.
I thank my God, Jesus every day for this awesome you
Baby I know you love me too.
Lord I worship You, I am not Lonely
I have You, I will love Betty.
I am faithful and true.
I lay down my life for her,
As I lay down my life for You.

Inspiration and/or reason:

'I Was Lonely' was written to acknowledge to God that I was comfortable being alone. Yet I knew His plans for me was NOT to remain alone. But the most important ingredient in being ready for Marriage is to realize you don't really have to and be comfortable with that idea. In other words, you must be a whole single person before you are ready to join with someone else. Otherwise, you develop an unhealthy dependance on your spouse that is unfair to you both.

I YEARN FOR YOU BETTY

Sitting. . .
I lay my hands on your legs
You look, welcome it & Smile
Your gestures puzzle me
But they are sweet—they are sweet.

You are with me
You burst with joy & love
You look tranquil on the outside
I gaze & shake my head
You are settled—you are at peace.

I can hold your hands
They die in mine
They have no other work to do
You love me with a squeeze
Baby your ways I love—your ways I love.

We walk together
We walk close together
We have strength to go the mile
You are proud & assertive
U & I we cover grounds—we cover grounds.

You are in Trinidad
These are but a memory
But you are a part of my heart

Come to me baby I miss you
I long for you—I yearn for you. . .

Inspiration and/or reason:

'I Yearn For You Betty' was written in anticipation of marrying this wonderful lady who 'receives' my touch and lights up. My love language is touch so that tells it all. Being physically close as in the same country, room or chair was all we could have done. But that is also all we needed.

"I'LL WAIT"

Right now it's raining. . .
On my life Baby
It is wet, dim, cold.
Movement minimal
I think of you Betty.
Feel like I am in Guyana
Miles away
By distance, by phone, by letter.
I mourn. . . with hope
I think of you Betty
Rain dampens my thoughts
The cold slows it down.
Your presence resident in my heart
It's like a link
Keeps me alive
Gives me hope
Someday will take me from here
Into your arms
By your side—close—airtight
In the air
Backdrop of Gray silhouette.
Bodies erect merge together
I kiss pass your lips- to your heart.
Your sexy figure [-you are sexy sweetheart, you heard me say it first,
you don't need another to tell you-].
I kiss your personality
I kiss your love for me

I kiss your love for God.
We ravish what is ours in each other
We drivel—we cry out for anticipation
For pain, love, ecstasy
Uncharted grounds.
Yet we're tunneling
Unknown skies
Yet we fly.
Foreign waters
Yet we sail.
New emotions
Yet we feel—deep, passion, wet, wild.
Betty I just miss you-
Funnel of love.
But on God, on You
I'll Wait.

Inspiration and/or reason:

'I'll Wait' was written on a rainy day. You know those kind of days makes you miss your loved ones even more. Guyana I am not from but serves as a reference to a place that always rains and is very far. It is a commitment to wait despite the temptations.

IN THE BEGINNING

In the Beginning
Ahh marriage—would be nice
But can't see it now.
Reluctant, Pushed,
I—Don't—Resist.
I love her ummm
Marriage is Honorable yes! Yes!!!
But when, I didn't see it.

Yeah sure she is in love with me
My baby, She's excited.
Why do you think this is God's Will?
I have not received this word!
Until I sense, hear, and feel—no Deal.
Surely character he reveal.
Love God—Foreign—Love me
This is my Wife to be.
Reminds me of the most insipid tea
Lord Adonia, open my eyes
That I may see who will it be. . . ..
"My son it is she"—Betty.

Inspiration and/or reason:

'In The Beginning' depicts the vail between being happily single,
the desire to marry and the question of if that prospect is right you.

IT SAYS I LOVE YOU

It says; Ephesians 5:25–28 says,

25 **Dwight,** love **Betty-Ann,** just as Christ also loved the church and gave Himself for her,
It says; 26 that He might sanctify and cleanse her with the washing of water by the word,
It says, 27 that He might present her to Himself a glorious wife, not having spot or wrinkle or any such thing, but that she should be nourished and cherished, holy and without blemish.
28 So **Dwight** ought to love his own wife **Betty-Ann** as his own body; for when he loves Betty-Ann he loves himself.

Now I say;
Can you hear it; in my voice?
Can you hear it; in this song?
I apologize for the ways and years I got it wrong.
But tonight is ours; our future STRONG.
In my arms, in my life is where you belong.

You are my object of my affection,
A vision of perfection.
Our love grows stronger through time,
As we learn to 'compliment' each other as a rhythm.
We will always have our kicks,
And solve more problems than Vicks.

I love you Betty-Ann **Esther** Bloodman.
I love you alone;

Flesh of my flesh, bone of my bone,
Now until I see God's Throne!

Inspiration and/or reason:

'It Says I Love You (Betty-Ann)' depicts a promise to love your partner right and forever. This kind of commitment was developed over time, with self-introspection and written in stone.

IT STARTS WITH ONE

You only need one to start a collection
The first anniversary is the time of our reflection.
We met in church, shook hands, and connected
I saw the spirit of light in us reflected.
The marriage, this love was then expected
Betty-Ann for Dwight
Dwight for Betty in God was selected.
To the altar, to the moon
We were carried. . .
Living in love since the day we got married.

Inspiration and/or reason:

"**It Starts With One**' is a commemoration of the 1st wedding anniversary. I like to mark special events with a special poem, however long or short it may be. You are welcomed to request a personal poem for any special occasion.

LAST NIGHT

Last night I was so disappointed and hurt
That I did not fully grasp your gifts and non-monetary worth.
But today as I went my way
It's immense shimmering beauty was revealed to me,
Not mentioning things you would say.
So, in tears of the heart, I would like to say,
Thank You for the watch and words.
I love you. . .
I guess the way to a man's heart is through his stomach,
And watches too;
I sincerely love you.

Inspiration and/or reason:

'**Last Night**' is about **conflict resolution**. I did not care for the birthday celebrations nor my gifts. I was justifiably upset. I 'WALKED' AWAY. I resolved it the next day.

LAY ON ME THE THING I SHOULD PRAY

Lay on My Heart Lord
The thing I should pray. . .
To touch someone's heart
To Worship You
In the right way.

Inspiration and/or reason:

'Lay on Me the Thing I Should Pray' is a simple, quick prayer for direction. Useful especially when there is encroaching darkness all around with little space to move and room to breathe.

"LOOK IN"

1

I am inviting you to look in,
Discover who I am,
Please, you must look in!
You cannot see it on the outside,
You will never see it without,
You must look in.

2

I am Complex,
A mystery to be discovered.
But the clues are inside,
So you must look in,
'The Skin' is a Hypocrite,
A master of camouflaging
the dominant role player.

3

But wait what are you doing?
Don't look with your eyes,
They cannot see—look in!
Use conversations, patience, opportunities. . .
And as you get to know me,
You will look beyond my skin
And see me.

Inspiration and/or reason:

'Look In' is another way to say 'don't judge a book by its cover'. Once invited to learn a person or thing, put prejudices on the back burner and 'look in' wholistically, and even creatively. Your findings will not be through the eyes of another whether it turns out to be the same opinion or not. It could be used to help quell racial, ethnic, religious and pollical issues too, **though not written at all with those in mind.**

'LORD FORGIVE ME FOR LOVING LIKE THIS'

Dwight   Betty

Lord   forgive
Me for   loving like this.
My potential is far   above what I mete out.
My bowels are violent,   but I keep 'them' calm.
What wickedness this is to hold back breath from
Her. To stifle a hold   society for they know
not that This is their   potential.
Lord God allow me   to relax, to feel,
to give huh,   to Love without
restrain, doubting,   investigation, fear.
To Love You, to Love   Myself, to Love Her
As the Sun rises it   forces newness in all
(these Two) that   is witnessing
it. Will   You
marry   Me
Betty

.

Inspiration and/or reason:

In sarcastically saying 'Lord Forgive Me For Loving Like This' due to seriousness of pure desire this poem was written. This is similar to the 'All My Life' heart-shaped poem. They are poetic not only in words but in their physical shape structure as well, i.e., heart shaped. They depict two people or hearts or souls coming together in conversation firstly. Speaking back and forth to each other. They are saying the same things, hoping and praying the same things whether they know it or not, realizing stages in love at the same time. As we also come together in soul, in heart, in spirit and of the body in marriage until we merge as one in every way, and you cannot tell us apart.

LOVE ME AT VALENTINE

Love me tender
Love me nice
You will always be the only love in my life.
Love me—wonderful
Love me sweet
Thinking about it make my heartbeat.

Inspiration and/or reason:

'Love Me At Valentine' is a Valentine's Day short poem to add to
and accent the celebration and gifts.

MERRY CHRISTMAS MOTHER

Christmas is a time
When we are a little kinder,
And so, my loving mother
I send you a reminder.

Inspiration and/or reason:

'**Merry Christmas Mother**' is a Mother's Day short poem to add to and accent the celebration and express yet another piece of love for my mother who did a great job raising us all by herself.

MY WIFE & MY WOMAN

My Wife. . .
She lies on my Chest.
Finally! our Wedding is here,
Our Honeymoon is now.
She feels Oh so good
The day we waited for
Blood, Sweat & Tears.
We smile and Groannn
AS our emotions unfold
Ummm we can release all.
Yesterday too much
But today All.
No restrained Actions,
No restrained Words,
No restrained Thoughts,
Just Bliss in Christ.
Working that which Is Seemly
Artistic & Instructive
Rough & Gentle
Loud & Soft
Long & Short
Here & There
Twisting & Turning
ALL positions—ANYWHERE
Scratching & rubbing
Violent & Tempered
Hurricane, Tornado, Hail, Thunderstorm, snow!!!

We are finally here. . .
We are one tonight. . .
We are married. . .

Yes Betty you are My **Woman** and I love you.
You know I am your man -you love me too.
I place my hands on your legs,
You rupture inside with welcome and a smile.
I Kiss Your Lips, you're glad to taste mine.
I look at you -oh so sublime.
I touch your heart, you touch mine
You've demand quality time.
My woman. . .
You hold my hand,
We walk over time's sand. . .
Loving me, loving you
Feet in step, heart in heart, hand in hand, we are One
I am your man, and you are:
My Woman.

Inspiration and/or reason:

'My Wife & My Woman' were two poems now morphed into one.
There are 2 reasons this was done. The 1st reason for doing this is
to highlight that your spouse should also be your girlfriend or boy-
friend even after marriage. Some things you did before marriage like
dating should continue after the wedding day for the health of the
relationship. The 2nd reason is a secret. You may ask; I may tell you.

"NONEXISTENT"

Sometimes it seems nonexistent
Oh baby you are so far away
I wonder if I have a girl friend
Or is this a dream.

When you call it becomes reality again
There is no place I can go and see you
I can't call you to come over
I can't pass you in the streets.

I try to be strong
How can anyone be stronger than love?
People I see make me say oh Betty
I constantly try, sweetheart I really try.

I maximize my moments
They are not complete without you
So I drag on, 'can't say I love you'
Can't turn inside out with emotions.

I do the most weeping
There is a flood inside you can't see
Touch me—I am moist with tears
I will love you all the years. . .

Inspiration and/or reason:

'Nonexistent' was written because I missed my girlfriend's physical presence. Yes, it was an overseas relationship for about 3 years. That should say it all. This poem should some of the challenges of overseas or long-distance relationship and the hope that keeps you both focused.

NOW MY KISS

Now my kiss means so much more
Then it was simply an open door.
Then it was foreign an exciting wonderland
But now you're forever in my hand.

Now my kiss means so much more
Its goodbye see you later when you walk out the door.
It's a sign that I need you and more.
It's comfort to my lifetime wife and friend
Assurance that I'll always be here
A promise that the kisses will never end.

Inspiration and/or reason:

'**Now My Kiss**' shows the transition. This transition is between the excitement of a young relationship where you are getting to know each other to a matured, marital relationship. By the way, 'kiss' is not necessarily that lips phenomenon but the principle idea of a kiss. . . Think about it, a kiss is just an expression of affection.

ONE NAME

We stand in worship
We stand in unity
Oh, Your presence
Oh, Your glory.
I now understand
Rejoicing in soft song
Bursting from our chest
Bursting from our bellies
Pouring through our mouths
Oh, the Love
Oh, the peace
Fulfilling, one with God
Vibrating, tottering
Between the point of body and pure spirit
One, one, one
As we behold—one name: Jesus.

Inspiration and/or reason:

'One Name' scratches the surface of corporate worship of Jesus
Christ. We all know that worship and worship of God cannot be
even near-fully captured with words. Any worship is something to
be experienced.

OUR HEARTS

Virtually everyone's hearts are halved
Therefore we seek keenly another half
One that fits the grooves and contours
And the figurative links of ours.
And when that identical half is found
they join firmly becoming one
With the adhesive time
The mender of all things.

In reality the spirits of married couples become one,
in a complex, mind-boggling manner.
Thus they dance together
In movements expressing love.
To the naked eye the above is called LOVE.

Inspiration and/or reason:

'Our Hearts' shows the figurative status of everyone's 'hearts' before and after finding real love. Hearts here is the real heart, the matching or help-meet soul. This poem has won hearts and competitions.

SHOULD I DO IT

Ahh! Look at it
Should I, do it?
How, how do I start?
Am I fulfilling this in vain?
And it is confronting me -
Lingering and malingering. . .
Wisdom Lord, should I pursue it?
Oh yeah! I must, but how?
My God help me,
BE with me and guide me,
For seeds of confusion is germinating,
And I can't waste my variables on this,
I must resolve this quickly,
I must establish my goal;
The everlasting light ahead. . .
Okay I know, I 've got it,
I know what and how to do it,
Thank you, Father, I'll do it right now!

Inspiration and/or reason:

'Should I Do It' is a play on making a or any decision by mental processing and prayer. Note that "I'll do it right now" can mean starting to plan because everything has a right time not necessarily a perfect time to be done.

TAKE CARE OF MY BODY

Take care of my body—precious
Remember you're one.
Take care of my heart
As long as it's single, we'll never part.
Care my head
Without it our love is dead.
Keep my Egyptian eyes
Their mystery I cannot despise.
Please care my 'delicious lips'
From them can flow tides of new tricks.
Let my right wash my left hand
I'll need to hold it when we become one.
Nurture my feet
In love we will walk carefully and neat.
I'll know who you love,
For when you take care of my body,
You'll be taking care of me.

Inspiration and/or reason:

'Take Care Of My Body' plays on the idea that spouses' bodies 'belong' to each other after married. This is 'coupled' with the idea that you are spiritually and physically one. It is a physical and relational admiration of my partner.

THE ICE CUBE

The ice cube lays in the cup so vulnerable. . .

He knows that he was a short time

So, he escapes partially by his sidekick, water vapor.

But he will not totally escape

For insulated plastic cup is putting on the heat. . .

So, he slowly laps into lazy, to and fro H2O.

Yes! Cup's heat is blocked by my heat,

insulated, level-headed Bro H2O,

Ohh no!

A human throw ice and his bro into large warm water which does not stir or flow.

Large water strips away ice, molecule by molecule—mercilessly!

And after being influenced by large water,

Those SAME molecules turn against ice striping his fabric away. . .

Surely ice will melt in the next three minutes or so,

But don't worry, he promises to be back tomorrow.

No matter what they do, it will not last

And ice's "Soul" essence lives on. . .

From the Present and the past!

Inspiration and/or reason:

'The Ice Cube' was conceived when eating one day in my mother's house. I threw some left-over ice in a cup of water in the kitchen. Inevitably the ice will melt in the water if they are not in a sub-zero environment. . .

THE MISSION, THE MAN

1

Christopher Columbus the mission, the man,

What was his, Spain's plan,

To be the first reach the West,

Little did they know they'll have to lay that trophy to rest.

2

Try they did to sail,

Many nights and days as the oceans wailed,

Ninety strong, 3 ships traveled far,

Guided by nothing but a compass, hope and star.

3

And just when they wanted to turn back,

12th October 1492, Bahamas stopped them dead in their track.

Indians they hoped, we finally found gold!

But Awakawa natives with only food and spices they could hold.

4

Was it hope, greed, or pride for Spain?

He continued on, gold for economic gain.

Although he did not get the country quite,

He did the same in Antigua right?

Inspiration and/or reason:

'The Mission, The Man' was done for one of my daughters for school. It is about Christopher Columbus, the real man, and his real mission. Yes, she got 100% marks for it.

THE MORE I LOVE GOD

The more I love God the more I love you Betty
My heart yearns for God He points me to you
Complete in Christ too & my 'help meet'.

Truly Betty I love you
When I look away I love you
I look to God He points me to you
I see our future in my eyes
I Miss You Sweetheart. . . huhh. . .

God gives me the strength to wait
The closer I go to Him
He strengthens me to love you
To do all His Will
To keep myself strong in Him
Gordosh Adonia.

Inspiration and/or reason:

'The More I Love God' was written because I learnt a trend by
experience. The more we love God and adapt His standards for us,
the more we can love each other. When we love each other, we are
loving God by His own words.

THE TWO PERFECTION

The moment I saw it I Knew
This is God's perfect number. . .
Seven
For you
And Seven
For me.
They ever shine like the stars in God's hands
Durable. . .
We are like them Betty-Ann
We are Better than they are.
As a symbol of God's perfection
Take it as I pose the Question. . .

Inspiration and/or reason:

True story, 'The Two Perfection' was written as a part of my elaborate engagement production. It describes the ring. Obviously, my plan worked, my goal achieved.

THINK ABOUT IT

Every time Sunday ends, I miss you
Because I know it might be two days
Before I see you again.
But how else would I know the longing I have for you?
So, I welcome and explore this happening in silent tears
I separate my emotions from my moments of love in action towards you. . .
And each time I think of you—of us 'hmmm'!
I realize:
I love you more than I do yesterday
And only half as much as I will
Love you tomorrow. . .
Think about it. . .

Inspiration and/or reason:

'Think About It' written to examine my feelings towards my girl-friend. Is it infatuation, or real love?

TRUE LOVE

Sometimes I feel sorry
For you just don't know
How much I love you
And the many ways to show.
Love destiny is saying something
I think you already know
That you're my true love
And our love will always grow.
Girl you must give me this much a chance
So, you and I can know
We are meant for each other
I'm sure your mutually anxious to know. . .
All it need is a simple try
Then destiny will show.

Inspiration and/or reason:

'True Love' fell in the perfect position right after the poem 'Think About It' which ponders whether I love this person or not. 'True Love' is the position where I now knew this was, well true love.

WHEN

When was the last time I felt,
That it just stuck me there:
"Someone loves me."
When was the last time I reclined on that thought. . .?
To know someone loves me—unconditionally?
When!. . . was the last time?
Then he whispers in my heart,
Every day of your life
Dwight, I love you with an everlasting love—
That will never part.

Inspiration and/or reason:

'When' was written in a 'love-eureka' moment. You know that moment when the truth of a situation truly 'hits home'? That 'When' moments is infinitely magnified when you know that person who loves you is God Almighty.

"WHEN YOU SAY"

When you say I love you, you're saying you will give your body to me
That sweet, beautiful waistline. . .
When you say I love you, you're saying you need me passionately
Even to just relax in your man's arms. . .
When you say I love you, you're pleased with my relationship with God
A Prophet, Priest & King to lead the family . . .
When you say I love you, you get weak in the knees
As a thought of me can render you. . .
When you say I love you, the comfort of Love overwhelms you
You never expected to be loved like this. . .
When you say I love you, you desire for me to hold you
Your whole body shivers. . .
When you say I love you, I want to caress you softly
To have you melt like butter. . .
When you say I love you, you're satisfied even with my presence only
We fall asleep in each other's arms. . .
When you say I love you, your spirit gets excited
You fall for me deeper. . .
When you say I love you, you yearn for me
You salivate at the mouth for a kiss. . .
When you say I love you, you wish I would reply & come good
I touch your soul with my words
Betty when you say I love you, I say I love you too
I. . . just. . . love. . . you.

Inspiration and/or reason:

'When You Say' is a caution and alert to what saying I LOVE YOU in certain contexts may mean. In my case, I knew it meant all of that expressed in the poem. It is with her I learned to 'say' I love you without flinching.

WITHIN ME

Time changes funder and funder
But it is not to wonder, don't ponder
For soon you will see
The love I kept for you, within me.

Inspiration and/or reason:

'Within Me', this short poem condenses the realities of a courtship of abstinence. You look forward to the fulfillment of all you could not do before marriage.

YOUR ARRIVAL

A rose bloomed to announce your birth
For essence was being added to the earth
I pray for many more years you'll stay
Happy Birthday.

Inspiration and/or reason:

'**Your Arrival**' is a short **poem to accent** my girlfriend's Birthday.

YOUR DESTINY

Everything I do
I fall deeper in love with you
As time goes by, our future flashes before my eyes
So, I just can't see why it can't be
Your destiny, to fall in love with me.

Inspiration and/or reason:

'**Your Destiny**' just as it said was a recognition that it was our destiny to be together. These are not just light words, but something undeniable happened to prove it to us. The thing about some destinies though is, you still have your part to play and do the necessaries to make it great.

YOUR PRAYERS

I'm ecstatically grateful you kept me in **your prayers**
I'll humbly elucidate gratitude Throughout my years. . .
And in case you ponder,
Your intercession helped to let God come down on me stronger.

I'll forever thank God for such a friend
And Jesus for intercepting me from that nasty end. . .
There is so much I can say to you
For helping to make my day every moment I pray
Lord maintain her spiritual insuperability
Afterall, of this nature is the body of Christ to be.

My hope is for these words to touch you in a special, powerful,
moving way,
And keep you gleaming infinitely graceful—
Especially Christmas Day.

Inspiration and/or reason:

'**Your Prayers**' was written in recognition that my wife to be prays
for me. It is an expression of love and gratitude to her and God.

YOU'RE PRICELESS

There is no fortune in losing a true love
Somethings are priceless.
I mean, what will it take for you to know I love you,
And what would you do to show me you love me too?
As you show me the act
I want you to see, you're special to me.
I adore your hypnotic eyes
They send love rays against which I can't immunize.
You're closer to me, than blood to my artery
Your intangible love at my feet
Gives more love and vigor than the food I can eat. . .
Ohhh your so sweet!
Yet you don't rot my teeth. . .
They shine as your spirit speaks with mine
"Let's get 'together' for 'time.'"
But enough with rhyme,
As I speak these words from the pages of my heart,
Washed pure with spring water,
Fossilize them in your heart,
For some day you will need to know,
There is no fortune in losing a true love;
_____ you're priceless. . .

Inspiration and/or reason:

'You're Priceless' is somewhat prophetic in hindsight; due to the
turbulence of life that will try to pressure you apart from each

other. It debates that we belong 'with each other' in THIS SIDE OF ETERNITY. You can place the name of the person who falls in this category on the dotted line in the last line of this poem.

Made in the USA
Middletown, DE
21 September 2024